The European Union

Julie Haydon

Rigby

www.Rigby.com
1-800-531-5015

Rigby Focus Forward

This Edition © 2009 Rigby, a Harcourt Education Imprint

Text © 2008 Julie Haydon
Published in 2008 by Nelson Australia Pty Ltd ACN: 058 280 149
A Cengage Learning company

1 2 3 4 5 6 7 8 374 14 13 12 11 10 09 08 07
Printed and bound in China

The European Union
ISBN-13   978-1-4190-3844-0
ISBN-10   1-4190-3844-3

Acknowledgments
The author and publisher would like to acknowledge permission to reproduce material from the following sources:
Photographs by AAP Image/AFP Photo/Gerard Cerles, p. 4; AAP Image/AP Photo/Vadim Ghirda, p. 19; AGE Fotostock, p.16; Harcourt Achieve/ ComStock Royalty-Free front cover (middle), pp.1, 23; Corbis, front cover (bottom), pp. 8-13, 17-8; Getty Images, p. 16/ AFP Photo, p. 20; iStockphoto.com/ p.7/ Matthew 71, p. 21; Jupiterimages, back cover, p. 15; Lonely Planet Publications © 2007, p. 6; Photolibrary, pp. 5, 7, 22-3.

The European Union

Julie Haydon

Contents

Chapter 1

THE EUROPEAN UNION

The European Union, or EU, is an organization made up of democratic European countries. EU countries are called member states. EU member states work together to give their citizens a better way of life.

The EU's political system is based on several treaties that are signed by the member states. The treaties set out the aims and rules of the EU. The EU doesn't replace European countries or their governments.

EU member states representatives voting at the European Parliament

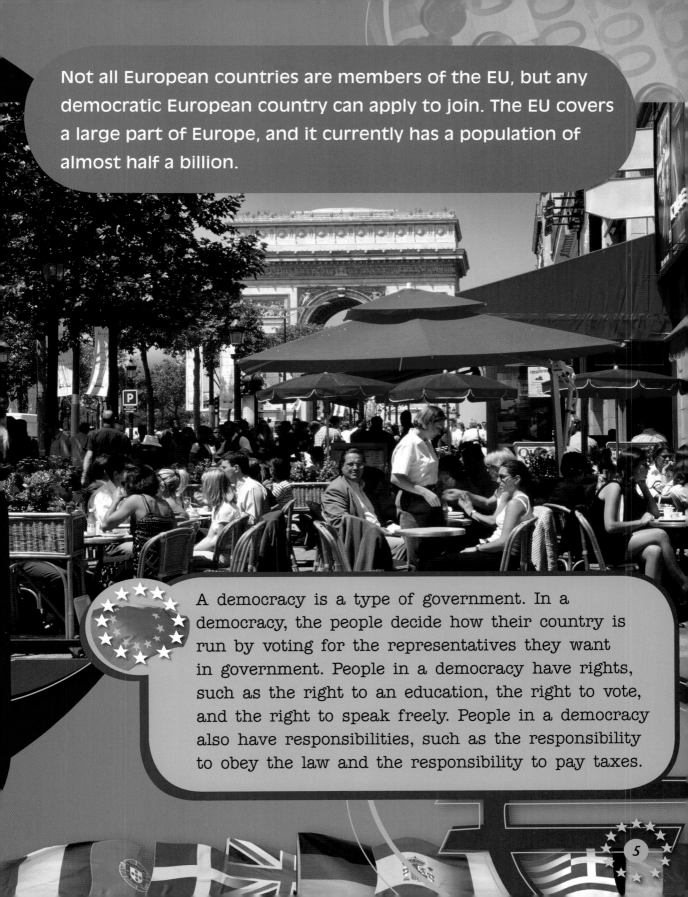

Not all European countries are members of the EU, but any democratic European country can apply to join. The EU covers a large part of Europe, and it currently has a population of almost half a billion.

A democracy is a type of government. In a democracy, the people decide how their country is run by voting for the representatives they want in government. People in a democracy have rights, such as the right to an education, the right to vote, and the right to speak freely. People in a democracy also have responsibilities, such as the responsibility to obey the law and the responsibility to pay taxes.

Chapter 2

THE MEMBER STATES

Twenty-seven countries are currently members of the European Union. They are Austria, Belgium, Bulgaria, Cyprus, Czech Republic, Denmark, Estonia, Finland, France, Germany, Greece, Hungary, Ireland, Italy, Latvia, Lithuania, Luxembourg, Malta, the Netherlands, Poland, Portugal, Romania, Slovakia, Slovenia, Spain, Sweden, and the United Kingdom.

the member states of the EU

European Union member states are committed to:

- democracy.
- peace.
- the rule of law.
- respect for human rights.

The EU has created a large, stable area in Europe, but it also aims to spread its values beyond its member states to create a more united and stable world.

Chapter 3

THE HISTORY

The first move toward the creation of the EU began after **World War II**. The war destroyed parts of Europe and millions of people died. Many people wanted to make sure that destruction like this never happened again.

In 1951 Belgium, France, Germany, Italy, Luxembourg, and the Netherlands signed a treaty that set up the European Coal and Steel Community (ECSC). The ECSC created a common market in coal and steel in the hope of promoting peace and cooperation between countries that were once enemies.

The ECSC was a success. Over time other treaties were written and more European countries signed them. This eventually led to the creation of the European Union in 1992.

The Treaty on European Union was signed in February 1992, creating the EU. The treaty was signed by 12 countries in Maastricht in the Netherlands. The treaty, also called the Treaty of Maastricht, went into effect in November 1993.

the Treaty of Maastricht

A treaty is a written agreement signed by two or more nations.

Chapter 4

THE INSTITUTIONS

European Union member states give some of their decision-making powers to shared **institutions**:

The Council of the European Union

The Council of the European Union is the EU's main decision-making institution. A politician from each member state goes to each council meeting. The council passes laws and makes decisions in areas such as transportation, industry, and the environment. It also votes on important issues, such as making changes to the treaties or allowing a new country to join the EU.

the European Parliament

The European Parliament

The European Parliament represents the citizens of the EU. The members of the Parliament are elected every five years. Along with the Council of the European Union, the Parliament passes EU laws. The Parliament and the Council of the European Union also share responsibility for approving the EU's budget.

The European Commission

The European Commission's job is to consider what is best for the EU. The commission has one member from every EU member state but must not be influenced by any country's government. The commission puts forward ideas for new EU laws and the EU budget, which the Council of the European Union and European Parliament then decide on.

a European Commission meeting

the 11th president of the European Commission, José Manuel Barroso

The European Council

The European Council is a regular meeting of the political heads of the EU's member states and the president of the European Commission.

The leaders talk about important issues in Europe and the world, and they decide the way forward for the EU. The European Council also settles issues that the Council of the European Union has been unable to agree on.

Chapter 5

THE CURRENCY

The euro is the currency of the European Union. Currently 12 EU countries use the euro. These countries are Austria, Belgium, Finland, France, Germany, Greece, Ireland, Italy, Luxembourg, the Netherlands, Portugal, and Spain. The area in which the euro is used is called the euro area. Other EU countries may join the euro area in the future.

EU countries using the euro

Finland

the Netherlands

Ireland

Belgium

Germany

Luxembourg

Austria

France

Portugal

Spain

Italy

Greece

The euro was introduced on January 1, 2002. It replaced the previous currencies of the 12 countries. There are eight **denominations** of euro coins and seven denominations of euro bank notes.

Chapter 6

LIVING IN THE EUROPEAN UNION

Citizens of the EU have many advantages. The EU created a single market, which means that people, goods, and services can move freely between EU countries. This can save time and money. The euro also makes it easy for people to compare prices and to buy and sell goods and services in different EU countries. EU citizens can live, work, or study in another EU country, too.

Some of the EU's budget is used to improve the way people live. This is done in many ways, such as creating jobs, teaching people new work skills, working to protect the environment, and fighting crime.

Chapter 7

JOINING THE EUROPEAN UNION

A country that applies to join the EU is called a candidate country. Before a candidate country can join the EU, it must meet the EU's entry requirements. A candidate country must be a democracy and have institutions that guarantee the rule of law and respect for human rights. A candidate country must also have a healthy economy and be able to apply EU laws.

Bulgaria became a member of the EU on January 1, 2007.

It can take up to ten years from the time a candidate country applies to join the EU to it becoming a member. All member states must agree to a candidate country joining the EU.

Chapter 8

THE SYMBOLS

Europe Day is May 9th. On this day in 1950, the idea for the creation of a united Europe was put forward by a European politician. Today Europe Day is celebrated across the EU as the EU's birthday.

the Eiffel Tower lit up for Europe Day

The European flag is a symbol of the European Union. It is also a symbol that Europe isn't divided and shares one identity. The flag features a circle of 12 gold stars on a blue background. The circle represents unity among the people of Europe.

The European Union has an anthem. The melody comes from the Ninth Symphony composed by **Ludwig van Beethoven** in 1823. The anthem has no words, and it does not replace the national anthems of the member states.

Ludwig van Beethoven

The motto of the European Union is "United in Diversity." The EU celebrates the diversity that exists in Europe— the different languages, cultures, and ethnic groups. The EU encourages people from different countries to work together for a better world.

Glossary

**Beethoven,
Ludwig van**   a German composer. Beethoven (1770–1827) is generally regarded as one of the greatest composers in the history of music.

denominations   currency amounts, usually for coins or bank notes

institutions   organizations

World War II   a world war fought between 1939 and 1945

Index